Allah Gives Us Food

Text written by Saniyasnain Khan
Illustrated by Siddhartha Mazumdar

Goodwordkidz

Goodword Books Pvt. Ltd.
1, Nizamuddin West Market, New Delhi 110 013
Tel. 4355454, 4356666 Fax 4357333, 4357980 E-mail: info@goodwordbooks.com

Who gives us good things to eat?

2

Allah gives us good things to eat.

Allah gave us the fields

and the farms.

This is a lush green field.
What do we grow in the fields?

We grow food grains and

8

vegetables in the fields.

9

Allah gives us

all kind of vegetables.

What do we rear on the farms?

We rear cattle and poultry on the farms.

Drinking milk makes us healthy.

14

From where do we get
the milk to drink?
Allah has made the cows
give us pure milk.

What do the trees in the orchards give us?

16

17

They give us
wonderful
fruits to eat.

Allah makes
all kinds of
fruits.

19

Allah keeps up our strength with plenty of food.

Let us praise Allah for His blessings.

Let us praise Allah for
the way He cares for us.

24